THE UTES

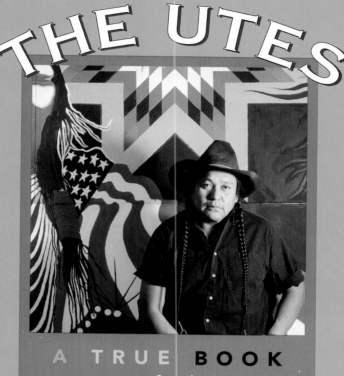

A TRUE BOOK

by

Alice K. Flanagan

Children's Press®
A Division of Grolier Publishing

New York London Hong Kong Sydney
Danbury, Connecticut

A Ute pattern

Reading Consultant
Linda Cornwell
Learning Resource Consultant
Indiana Department
of Education

Visit Children's Press on the Internet at:
http://publishing.grolier.com

Library of Congress Cataloging-in-Publication Data

Flanagan, Alice K.
 The Utes / by Alice K. Flanagan.
  p.   cm. — (A true book)
 Includes index.
 Summary: Presents the history, society, and culture of the Utes.
 ISBN 0-516-20455-6 (lib. bdg.)   0-516-26386-2 (pbk.)
 1. Ute Indians—Juvenile literature. [1. Ute Indians. 2. Indians of North
America.] I. Title. II. Series.
E99. U8F583   1998
978'.0049745—dc21   97-15089
                                                      CIP
                                                      AC

CURR

Contents

People known as the Fremont carved images into stone hundreds of years ago.

Descendants of an Ancient People

Once, the ancestors of the Utes (YOOTS) roamed freely throughout the Rocky Mountains of Colorado, as well as parts of Utah, New Mexico, and Arizona. Scholars believe they may have been the Fremont (FREE-mont) people. The Fremont people were living in the mountains and deserts of the southwestern United States about 10,000 years ago. Their rock art is some of the finest in the Southwest.

The Fremont and their Ute descendants lived in small family groups. They followed deer, mountain goats, and antelope from season to season. Eventually, these animals became the Utes' main source

The Utes relied on hunters to provide food, as this rock carving (left) shows. Occasionally, the Utes grew crops such as corn (right).

of food and clothing. To their animal diet, Utes added a variety of wild foods such as roots, seeds, nuts, and berries. They also hunted small game such as lizards and rabbits. From time to time, Utes

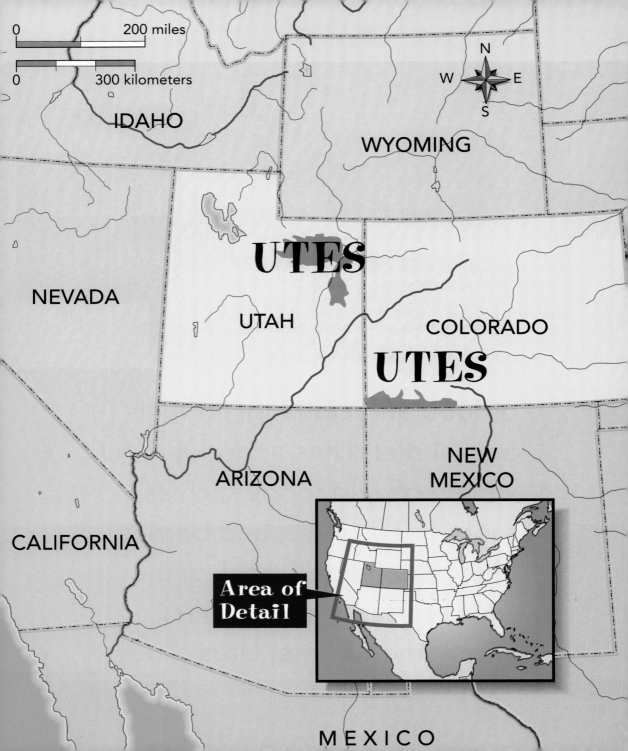

planted and harvested crops of corn and beans.

The word Ute comes from an Indian name meaning dwellers in the tops of the mountains. White settlers named the state of Utah after the Utes. In the 1860s and 1870s, the U.S. government forced the Utes onto areas of land called reservations. Today, most Ute Americans still live on reservations in Colorado and Utah.

Deer and Bison Hunters

The early Utes traveled and hunted on foot. In late fall, families left the mountains. They moved south with the deer, elk, and antelope in search of warmer, sheltered areas along rivers. There they spent the winter. In early

The Utes spent their winters in the sheltered areas along rivers.

spring, families joined each
other for antelope, deer, and
rabbit drives and for rare trips
to the Great Plains to hunt
bison (buffalo). For a few days

Every spring, Utes still come together to celebrate the Bear Dance.

in the spring, they gathered for the Bear Dance. Then, families returned to their summer hunting grounds in the mountains.

Each family had its own hunting and gathering area

and was familiar with others' areas. Everyone usually kept within their own boundaries. They respected each family's right to a particular hunting ground or a favorite food-gathering site.

In the summer, the Utes lived in the mountains.

Ute Homes

A thousand years ago, the Fremont people lived close to an advanced civilization called the Anasazi (ana-SA-zee). The Fremonts shared many similar customs with their Anasazi neighbors, such as living in pit houses and adobe (sun-dried clay) houses, weaving

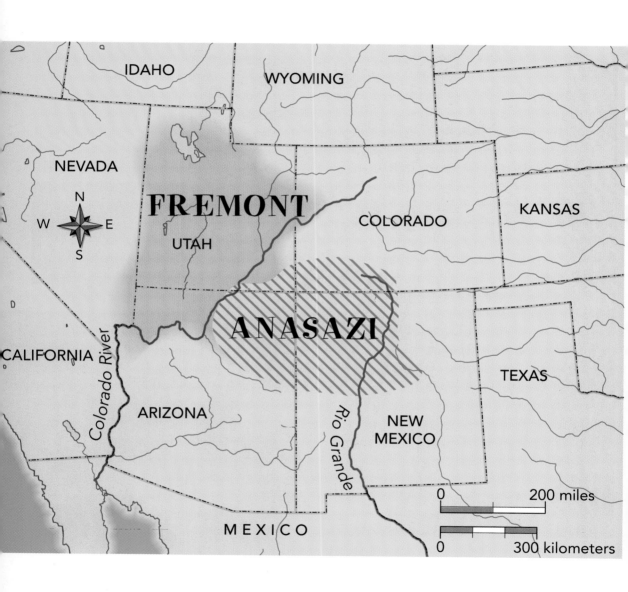

IDAHO

WYOMING

NEVADA

FREMONT

COLORADO

KANSAS

UTAH

Colorado River

ANASAZI

CALIFORNIA

ARIZONA

Rio Grande

NEW
MEXICO

TEXAS

MEXICO

0   200 miles

0   300 kilometers

A Ute blanket
(left) and
wedding basket
(below)

baskets, and painting pottery. Today, modern Ute designs on baskets and pottery show the influence of the Anasazi.

Over time, Utes began living in small, round dwellings called wickiups. Wickiups were made from a cone-shaped frame of poles covered with branches and grasses.

When Utes had contact with tribes living on the Great Plains, families began living in tipis, which they made from

After spending time on the Great Plains, the Utes began to live in tipis.

elk or buffalo hides. In 1868, the U.S. government forced the Utes to live on reservations. Then the Utes made their tipis from heavy cotton cloth provided by the U.S. government. Today, Ute families live in modern homes, like other Americans do. However, tipis are still used during special celebrations.

Today, Utes live in modern houses.

Family Life

In ancient times, Ute families were small—a husband and wife, their children, and sometimes elderly grandparents. Elders made important decisions and were treated with great respect. Eventually, when the size and number of families increased, the Utes

Elderly Utes are greatly respected by the rest of the tribe.

organized into seven groups called bands.

In each band, Ute women were in charge of building and maintaining the dwellings.

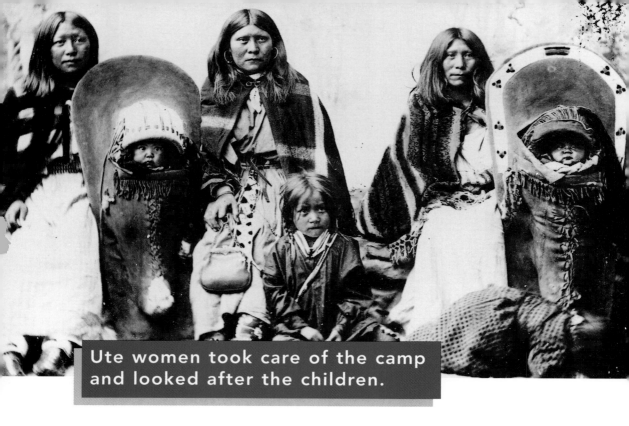

Ute women took care of the camp and looked after the children.

They made the household utensils and clothing, cooked the meals, looked after the children, and did most of the work when camps were moved. Men were responsible for hunting, fighting, and raiding enemy territory. They made the weapons and the ceremonial objects. Usually, they also conducted the ceremonies.

Ute men hunted and waged war on enemy tribes.

Dancing with

The Bear Dance has been a Ute custom since ancient times. Each year, in March, when bears left their winter dens and the spring hunting season began, Ute families gathered for the Bear Dance. The gathering was a time of prayer and celebration. It also gave people a chance to share news, trade items, and meet future

The Bear dance is led by a singer, who leads other couples in the dance.

the Bear

husbands and wives. Today, the Bear Dance is still an important tradition. Everyone is welcome to attend this social event that celebrates spring.

According to Ute legend, the Bear Dance began when a man from the tribe had a special dream. He saw a bear shuffling back and forth as if it were dancing. The bear taught the man how to do the dance and sing for it. The man returned to his people and taught them the dance. Since then, every spring, the Utes have been performing this dance.

Horses, Raids, and Warfare

Between 1630 and 1640, the Utes obtained horses from Spaniards living in Pueblo country, which is now the state of New Mexico. The horse gave the Utes their first opportunity to hunt large herds of buffalo. Soon

Ute warriors often posted lookouts to watch for approaching enemies.

the buffalo became their chief source of food. From buffalo, the people made tipi covers, blankets, glue, rope, toys, bows and arrows, drums, carrying bags, and clothing.

Utes made moccasins from soft elk or deer hide. They also used buffalo hide and kept the hair on the inside.

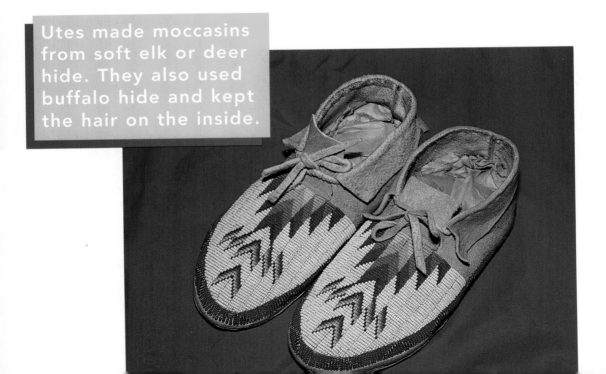

Utes adopted the headdress common to the Great Plains Indians.

Ute family life changed after the arrival of the horse. People began living together in large bands and sharing food and responsibilities. They adopted many of the clothing styles and customs of the Great Plains Indians.

With the aid of horses, hunting was easier and riders traveled greater distances. Soon, hunting parties became a part of daily life. When Ute hunters crossed into enemy territory, they often fought warriors of other tribes for food and supplies. Eventually, warfare became a normal part of Ute tribal life.

Ute war leaders were treated with great honor and respect. Whatever Ute war-

A modern
Ute war
dancer

riors took from their enemies
in battle, they gave away to
members of the tribe during
victory celebrations.

Sometimes, they traded what they had won for other things. The more prizes a warrior acquired in battle and gave away, the greater importance he had in the tribe. Although elders always held a place of importance, war leaders and chiefs controlled such activities as camp moves, hunts, raids, war parties, and dances. All individual matters in the bands, however, were decided by each family.

Vanishing Homelands

In 1848, the United States acquired the southwestern United States from Mexico, including New Mexico and all of Colorado where the Utes lived. When gold was discovered near Denver, Colorado, in 1859, thousands of gold seekers poured in from the

East. The Utes tried to keep outsiders away from their land, but there were too many of them. In 1868, after many battles, the Utes signed the first of many agreements (treaties) giving much of their land to the U. S. government.

The United States chose a Ute leader named Ouray to speak on behalf of his people because he could speak both English and Spanish. By signing agreements with the U.S.

OURAY   UTE CHIEF.

765

Ute leader Ouray hoped to save the best land for the Utes.

government, Chief Ouray thought he could save the best part of his people's land. But he soon learned that it would not turn out that way. Ouray said: "The agreement that an Indian makes to a United States treaty is like the agreement that a buffalo makes with his hunters when pierced with arrows. All he can do is lie down and give in."

Because Ouray was not chosen as chief by a Ute council

of elders, he was never accepted as a chief of the tribe. But Ignacio was chosen as chief of the Ute Mountain Utes. And he remained so all of his life.

Into the Twenty-first Century

Today, the Ute tribe rents much of its land to outsiders. It makes money from the sale of oil, gas, and minerals that U.S. companies mine from the land. The Southern Ute tribe runs a casino where people gamble money on

Today, the Southern Utes run a casino for tourists.

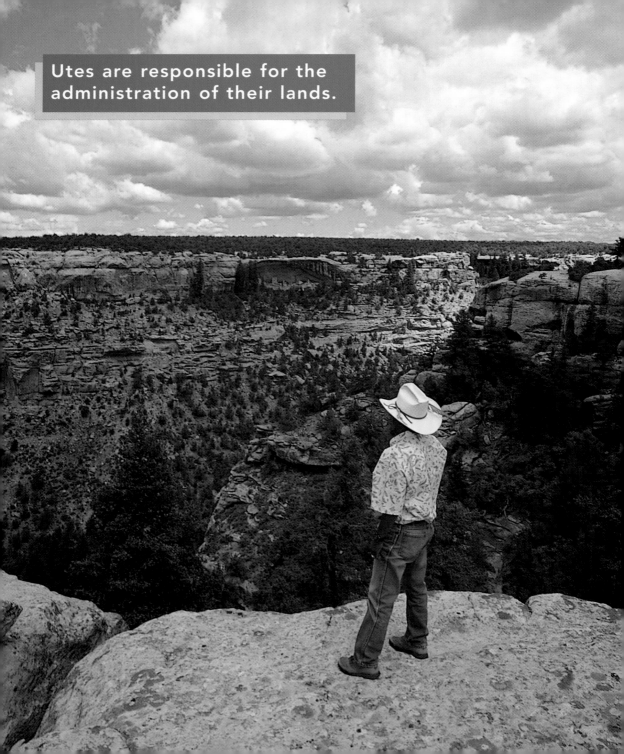

Utes are responsible for the administration of their lands.

games of chance. Some Utes
farm and raise livestock on
the reservation. Many live in
neighboring cities where
there are jobs and opportuni-
ties that the reservation
doesn't offer.

The Ute tribal council is
responsible for the welfare of
its members on the reservation. It uses tribal funds and
money from the U.S. government to provide courts,
police protection, housing,

health care, educational pro-
grams, streets and roads, fish
and wildlife regulations, and
recreation.

As Americans, Utes play an
active role in the affairs of
their country. But they are
also proud of the traditions
that make them Utes. To their
children, they offer the best
of both traditions as the Utes
enter the twenty-first century.

Utes rely on their proud heritage to meet the challenges of the future.

To Find Out More

Here are some additional resources to help you learn more about the Utes:

Books

Doherty, Craig A. &
  Katherine M. **Ute.**
  Rourke, 1994.

Fradin, Dennis. **Sea to
  Shining Sea: Colorado.**
  Children's Press, 1993.

Fradin, Dennis. **Sea to
  Shining Sea: Utah.**
  Children's Press, 1996.

Lyback, Johanna R. **Indian
  Legends.** Tipi Press,
  1994.

Miller, Jay. **American
  Indian Families.**
  Children's Press, 1996.

Miller, Jay. **American
  Indian Festivals.**
  Children's Press, 1996.

Organizations and Online Sites

Anasazi Archaeology
http://www.swcolo.org/ Tourism/ArchaeologyHome. html

An exciting site that displays several pages of Anasazi ruins.

Archaeological Sites of the Southwest
http://cac.psu.edu/~ghb1/ anasazi.html

A site that lists southwestern American Indian ruins and offers information about the people who lived there.

Capitol Reef National Park
http://www.nps.gov/care/ petpull.htm

Discover Fremont rock art at this National Park site.

Early Man of Utah
http://www.surweb.org/ surweb/sandbox/teachers/ nmehs.htm

This site concentrates on the ancestors of modern tribes in the Southwest.

Fremont Indian State Park
http://www.infowest.com/ fremont/

A state park site with information and photographs about the Fremont people.

The Heard Museum: Native Cultures and Art
http://hanksville.phast. umass.edu/defs/ independent/Heard/

Explore exhibits on American Indian Art in the Southwest.

Indian Ruins of the Southwest
http://seamonkey.ed.asu. edu/swa/anasazi.html

Site that lists and describes Indian ruins in the southwestern United States.

Native American Navigator
http://www.ilt.columbia. edu/k12/naha/nanav.html

A general site with hundreds of links to topics on Native Americans.

Important Words

adobe muddy mixture that is dried and used as bricks

ancestors people who came before

band group of Ute families living together

pit house dwelling built into the ground

potter person who works with clay to make pots or bowls

raid a small, usually secret, attack to steal things from another tribe

reservation land set aside for American Indian tribes by the U.S. government

wickiup Ute dwelling made from a cone-shaped frame of poles covered with branches and grasses

Index